BEAUTIFUL DAY

The Day You Were Born Was a
Beautiful Day

THE STORY

MICHELE JOHNSON & LEAH MILLER

WestBow
PRESS®
A DIVISION OF THOMAS NELSON
& ZONDERVAN

Scripture quotations marked (NIV) are taken from the Holy Bible, New International Version®, NIV®. Copyright © 1973, 1978, 1984, 2011 by Biblica, Inc.™ Used by permission of Zondervan. All rights reserved worldwide. www.zondervan.com The "NIV" and "New International Version" are trademarks registered in the United States Patent and Trademark Office by Biblica, Inc.™

Scripture quotations marked MSG are taken from THE MESSAGE, copyright © 1993, 1994, 1995, 1996, 2000, 2001, 2002 by Eugene H. Peterson. Used by permission of NavPress. All rights reserved. Represented by Tyndale House Publishers, Inc.

Scripture quotations are taken from the Holy Bible, New Living Translation, copyright ©1996, 2004, 2007, 2013, 2015 by Tyndale House Foundation. Used by permission of Tyndale House Publishers, Inc., Carol Stream, Illinois 60188. All rights reserved.

Scripture quotations taken from the Amplified® Bible (AMP), Copyright © 2015 by The Lockman Foundation Used by permission. www.Lockman.org

WestBow Press books may be ordered through booksellers or by contacting:

WestBow Press
A Division of Thomas Nelson & Zondervan
1663 Liberty Drive
Bloomington, IN 47403
www.westbowpress.com
1 (866) 928-1240

Because of the dynamic nature of the Internet, any web addresses or links contained in this book may have changed since publication and may no longer be valid. The views expressed in this work are solely those of the author and do not necessarily reflect the views of the publisher, and the publisher hereby disclaims any responsibility for them.

Any people depicted in stock imagery provided by Getty Images are models, and such images are being used for illustrative purposes only. Certain stock imagery © Getty Images.

ISBN: 978-1-9736-2342-7 (sc)
ISBN: 978-1-9736-2343-4 (hc)
ISBN: 978-1-9736-2341-0 (e)

Library of Congress Control Number: 2018903521

Print information available on the last page.

WestBow Press rev. date: 04/25/2018

We dedicate this book to our moms—the women who made us.

To my mom, who loves her children with her whole being and who will positively kill me for putting her picture in this book. Mom, I love you for a billion reasons.

—Leah

To my momma, who taught me how to love with all the passion the world could hold. Thank you for showing me how to be bold, fierce, and passionate and how to live a life worth remembering. Love you. I will see you again.

—Chele

Contents

Contents

Preface

We're two ordinary girls who were living ordinary lives until the summer of 2013. That summer, through a series of events and the leading of the Holy Spirit, we found ourselves making a quick exit off Ordinary Lane and merging onto Extraordinary Beltway. We're the cofounders of Beautiful Day Foundation, which celebrates thousands of birthdays in elementary schools and serves hundreds of widows. Beautiful Day Foundation is our baby who, in spite of us and because of God's grace, is getting bigger every day.

This book has been therapy for us, a formal process we have gone through to connect the dots of us pre–Beautiful Day Foundation and post–Beautiful Day Foundation. Sometimes, life can move so quickly that it's hard to stop and take note of how something went from a small idea to a real foundation that is helping real people.

This preface allows us, the authors, to explain how this book was written. It was authored by two people, Michele Johnson and Leah Miller. This preface was written by both of us as were the first and last chapters. But in the rest of the book, we take turns writing the chapters, and the author of each is noted at the beginning of the chapter. We hope this is as clear as mud. Ready? Let's get started.

Leah: Early on, the discussion began about how to list our names on the cover of this book. I know it was a funny place to begin this journey seeing we didn't actually have a book at that point, but we just couldn't decide. Should we alphabetize our names on the cover by our first names? Last names? Where is my *AP English Writing Style* textbook from 1992? I wonder if my sophomore English teacher is still awake at this late hour.

Michele: Did you notice? Two people in fact authored this book. I know, I know—that's so new age, so trendy. All the cool kids are doing it. Well, they will be doing it eventually. Could coauthoring become the new vaping?

Leah: *Beautiful Day: The Story* is equally authored by me, Leah Miller, and my ride-or-die friend Michele Johnson. I feel this dual authoring thing is so out there that we better cool it down in some way. Will this help? No animals were harmed in the coauthoring of this book.

Michele: Both of us wrote this book. There was no other way to tell this story, to release it in an organic, authentic, and accurate way. We had such conviction to share this journey in written format together.

Leah: Michele and I do a fair amount of public speaking together, so we channeled our speaking style for this book. This book is structured so that the story is told piece by piece, each of us telling a piece from our perspective and smoothly going back and forth between us to paint all the colors of this story.

Michele: Leah wrote the word *smoothly* so confidently, didn't she? I sure hope she's right. Let's do this.

Meet Leah

Michele and I talked about writing this book for months before sitting down to do it. I admit that I thought it would look quite different from what it does. I thought surely there would be a magic fairy that would start doing my family's laundry and grocery shopping once I began typing words. Do authors have to bleach their own bath rugs during the actual authoring?

I thought I would have all the silence I'd need to get my thoughts, feelings, amusements, and shenanigans out of my head and onto paper. I imagined there would be a buffet of brain food always at my disposal. Uh, no. That ain't at all how this went down.

Thanks to our awesome husbands and patient kids, we did steal away to hotels in undisclosed locations for a few weekends to write. Once we got through all the paparazzi, we would check into the hotel under aliases. Michele chose the name Michelle Johnson. Did you see what she did there? She added an *l* to her first name. So clever! I used the name Violet Casablanca. Obviously.

We would head to our room, plug in our laptops, and write and write and write. The bathroom mirror was hardly used on those trips. No Chi hair straightener or fancy mascara needed on those glamorous weekends. But I'll be honest—there were teeth-whitening strips. Always. Typing words while whitening teeth somehow just felt right. If we don't sell any copies of this book, it will not have been a waste. We'll still have bright, shiny-white teeth.

Forming a nonprofit foundation? Writing a book? Eating kale? I have to admit that I had never thought I would be doing such things, but here I am. I've heard a sweet voice calling me to these things (minus the kale), and I desperately want to walk down roads that God points to. So new friends, will you go with me on this journey? Like going to the ladies' room at a fancy restaurant, it'll be an easier journey if it's in good company. This will be a journey of what I have tasted and seen since scales fell off my eyes a few years ago.

Speaking of not journeying alone, Michele Johnson (the real one, not the alias), has been right there through some of the coolest days of my life. God saw fit to put me on the windiest, craziest, longest path with her, and it's been my honor. You know those pure and good friendships you run into too rarely in life? Yup. It's one of those.

If you stay on this journey with us and read all we have written, you'll see how our friendship was part of a larger plan. This girl is the real deal—a visionary and a huge dreamer, but those traits pale in comparison to her hunger to seek her Lord with her whole heart. Michele wants no stone in her life hidden from her Creator. No matter how painful it is, she wants Him to search her and mold her into His exact plan for her. It's beautiful and inspiring.

Our families have now been woven so tightly and beautifully together that there's real strength there. I'm terribly and forever thankful.

Michele and I know without a doubt that the Beautiful Day Foundation would not have been possible or nearly as fun without our core team. Our people. Our tribe. Our wolf pack.

Our kindred sisters (and brothers). Our posse. We have a core tribe whose members said yes before this baby could even hold up its head. They said yes when there was only an idea to say yes to. They are Cheryl Imel, Telise Ensey, Corey Ensey, Melissa Ray, Aaron Ray, Kailey Wellington, Parker Wellington, Geoff Johnson, Che Miller, Jan Palovik, Paula Toler, Kimber Budowsky, Debbie Savage and Gena Webb. How in the world did we get so lucky?

Running up this hill with this group is way better than winning the lottery! I have a constant running group text with many of these girls, so it's as if we're always in a full-blown, Beautiful Day meeting. I'm the luckiest girl to be doing anything at all with these girls much less living out my heart's desires.

> *The next best thing to being wise oneself is*
> *to live in a circle of those who are.*
> —C. S. Lewis

To Ava and Ruby, my daughters. You girls are the coolest gifts ever given to me, and being your momma is a billion times more fun than I ever dreamed it would be. You gals are the real deal; you love people like crazy. I can't wait to see your life stories unfold! I've joked for years that you girls are my tiny business partners. I always gave you that title when I walked into an important meeting with you on my hip. It's been true ever since I met you girls. You gals are the coolest! Thank you, kids, for understanding that kindness matters in this life and that how we treat others counts in the hugest ways.

I pray that Jesus will use all the raw materials Daddy and I have been putting in your lives to build something extraordinary for His kingdom. I pray a life full of the Lord's favor over you gals. Thank you for letting me be on your team.

To my husband—this dude is a solid yes. He was a yes to Beautiful Day right from the beginning. As Beautiful Day has grown and grown, he has been a yes. At the hint of Michele and me writing a book, he was a solid yes. In fact, our writing this book may have been his idea in the first place. Che Miller has cheered me on from the beginning, and he's done backflips with his schedule to give me space to do what I was called to do. He has jumped in with both feet to all that Beautiful Day does and was super-patient when his dry cleaning was stacked nearly to the ceiling in our closet rather than actually at the dry cleaners.

We have been doing life together since we were sixteen, and he's been a yes and a champion all these years. This dude knows how to love, serve, support, laugh, and protect all in *huge* ways and better than any human I've ever met. Being his wife is so much stinkin' fun! Thank you, baby.

I cannot write this introduction without thanking some other women, people who have inspired me whether they knew it or not. Michele and I discovered that we have this uncanny ability to kind of, sort of, accidentally bully amazing women into mentoring us. It's not mean bullying. Is *stalking* actually the word I mean here? Jan Palovik, Pam Dobbins, Sandy Stewart, and Carole Maxfield—you four ladies were probably six months into mentoring us before you even know what had happened. Michele and I love all four of you deeply and truly. You have loved us right where we are, and you pour buckets and buckets into us so freely. You always point our eyes up, and we are crazy thankful!

Then there are women I don't know personally but who inspired me with their written words. Funny, smart, witty, Bible-educated women are blazing the path for Jesus-loving women to say yes to the life He made for them and to say yes to do what He has invited them to do. I cannot write my words without acknowledging these women for theirs. These ladies' words inspired and energized me at all the right times: Ann Voskamp. Angie Smith. Jen Hatmaker. Lisa Bevere. Christine Caine. Jenny Allen. Maria Goff. Thank you, authors and speakers, for saying yes to sharing what you had tasted and seen.

So here we go. Want to get started? Let's agree to let this unfold and see what we see with no judgments. A professional writer I am not. I wish I could read this book aloud to you in my voice with all my verbal inflections and hand gestures. Once immediately prior to a long road trip that was set to begin at 4:00 a.m., I downloaded Amy Poehler's audiobook *Yes Please!* Hearing her voice read her own book was beyond fabulous and made driving down the highway at 4:00 a.m. way less lame. Amy is amazingly hilarious, and hearing her laugh at her own funnies made her funny even funnier. You know people who write better than they speak? I don't think I'm one of them, so you'll have to imagine my voice as you read my heartfelt words. Wait. I think that's how reading books works in every case. You know what I mean.

Michele and I wanted to write this book, but taking the next step can be hard and scary. Let's do it anyway.

Meet Michele

I kind of always wanted to write a book. How pretentious does that sound? I know, I know. I feel weird even telling you that, but it's true. I never really knew what the book would be about, but that's how God always talks to me. He gives me these tiny giant things, and I just live with them until they happen. More on that later.

My personality is big. Big. I have been known to accidently stomp on someone while just saying hi to him or her. I often have to walk myself through taming my personality down so I don't scare smaller personalities. I have been known to come in a little hot. I can totally relate to Peter. For real. It's okay, Peter. I probably would have cut his ear off too. I am always a yes even if I'm not completely prepared. I may not be prepared, but I'm ready. I have been told that prison is full of people with my personality type.

Even with this big ol' personality, you won't believe it, but I am a friend, sister, daughter, mom, business owner, daughter-in-law, niece, and wife. Not in that order. I'm not actually sure what order they go in, but I'm certain of all my titles. I take them seriously and am proud of them all. That last one means I have a husband, and that's a title he's earned.

This man, my husband. I could tell you a million details about us—how we met on the seventh-grade playground and how we fell in love. Or I could sum up our entire relationship with one story. Beaver nuggets.

We were headed to Houston from our home in Duncan, Oklahoma, to visit my parents when my mom was receiving chemo at MD Anderson. We loved stopping at Buc-ee's. If you don't know, Buc-ee's is the Arnold Schwarzenegger of convenience stores. Their mascot, logo, or hero is a beaver named Buc-ee. Clever, right? Stopping at Buc-ee's was always a highlight of our drive. I couldn't go inside that time because I was breastfeeding Sam. In the car. (If I were reading this aloud right now, I'd have screamed that last sentence as if it were Geoff's fault.) Anywho, I'd asked Geoff to get me a snack. Simple enough.

This guy, the leader of our family, the one I had chosen as my person for the rest of my life, came out of this bountiful store with farking beaver nuggets! That's what it read on the package. Beaver nuggets. *Ugh!* Now mind you, I'd never had beaver nuggets. I'd never even heard of them. But I knew I wouldn't like them. It was a habit of mine to say I want a snack but give no other details while I'm nursing a baby in the car by myself and wanting the most perfect and glorious snack you could imagine. I want it to be magical and perfect and exactly what I want. "I have no idea what it is exactly, but I want you to pick it out. Go."

After I threw my hissy fit about not wanting the beaver nuggets and crawled back into the front seat where nonbreastfeeding people belonged, I reluctantly and against my better judgment tried the stupid beaver nuggets. And the inevitable happened. They were awesome! They really were quite glorious in a can't-stop-eating-them way.

This is us. He knows me. He knows what I want before I want it. This has been our pattern of life since we were sixteen. It works.

He's a rock. A patient rock. He never says anything that isn't the truth. He will not agree or even guide you in any direction unless he believes it in his core. His commitment to loyalty and honesty is unmatched. He is a stable and safe place for me to always land. I often describe our relationship as me being the balloon full of helium and he is the one holding my string. He lets me fly just high enough but never lets go. There's no telling where I would be without him. Probably in an orange jumpsuit.

My babies. My most favorite job is being the momma of Ava and Sam. I know them better than they know themselves. I look forward to shaping and guiding and making fun of them for the rest of their lives.

So there it was. There I was. Taking the next step to writing a book.

My biggest fear about writing this book was that people would ask, "Who does she think she is? Does she think people really want to read her story?"

God has shown me so much about myself through this. While on the outside I am an almost a guaranteed yes, the inside needs work.

This is probably why God gave me a partner, a colleague, a collaborator, a sojourner. Not everyone gets a teammate in this field of interest, but I've been blessed many ways by Leah Miller. You'll soon find out that I lost my momma. That left a huge, gaping hole in my life. If you still have your momma, it's impossible for you to know how many questions you might ask her in any one week. Please don't misunderstand; Leah has not taken my momma's place. She couldn't possibly do that. She doesn't even want to.

But ... but ... I needed and still need a woman to bounce parenting techniques off of and changes in my heart and how to clean the tile floors and why this rash on my face won't go away.

Leah Miller has shown me how to love in tiny but huge ways. I have stood by and watched her throw a baby shower for a girl she'd just met. I've watched her make countless meals for people whom she may or may not have known. She loves my kids as if they were her own, and she shares my pride in them. I'm so excited for you to get to know her through this book.

Come with us on this journey of how God whispered to us and gave us the courage to say yes to the next step again and again.

1

The Pull of a Tragedy

Michele: "So do you think it was fate that you two met?" That question. Man. It rocked us! What made this local news reporter ask that question? We were being casually interviewed in an elementary school cafeteria by a local news reporter when we were asked that question for the first time. We had been doing Beautiful Day for three years, and no one had ever asked us that. *How do we answer this?* I asked myself. Leah was so quiet. Tearfully quiet.

I answered, "Yeah, I guess so."

We had met because Leah's husband and I were classmates in a local leadership class. After a couple of meetings, he said, "You and my wife would get along." I guess that was because we seemed so similar to him.

What you don't know is that Leah's husband is Dr. Che Miller, a general and vascular surgeon, and I'm a business owner as well as a mom and a wife. How could we have anything in common? Plus, I had plenty of friends.

1

Leah: The first I had heard of Michele was when Che suggested we go on a double date to Oklahoma City with a girl from his leadership class and her husband, Geoff. "Josh? Jeff? Goff?" I spent thirty minutes prior to our date trying to create clever ways to remember how to pronounce his name correctly. I decided on "Joff" Yes, I could remember that his name was pronounced "Joff." I also made a mental note to research who named someone Geoff and pronounces it Joff.

Che and I agreed that in a pinch during the evening, we would refer to Michele's husband as "Captain," "Chief," or "Cowboy." And no, I don't want to talk about my husband's brutally mispronounced name. We're talking about Geoff here.

Michele: So we went on a double date. It was perfect. We drove to Oklahoma City and ate at a fondue restaurant called The Melting Pot; nothing breeds a new friendship like a meal of raw meat served on a platter right in front of you. We went to a traveling Broadway show, *9 to 5*—great show. To my surprise, Dolly Parton did not play herself. I can honestly say that I liked Leah Miller very much and could see us being great friends. But, *meh*.

Leah: I remember us dropping them off at their house and feeling sad that the date was over. Michele was funny and crazy about her husband, two things I value in a girlfriend. We vowed to do this again.

Michele: Somewhere between the cooking of the raw meat and a sunny fall day months later, a super-dark cloud had fallen on my family. A terrible sickness had come for my momma. On August 15, 2011, she was diagnosed with stage-4 Non-Hodgkin's Lymphoma. What is that? Cancer, y'all. The only reason I knew it was cancer was because the business card the doctor left me read "Oncologist." For the record, I hate capitalizing that name. Washington, DC, Celine Dion, Potbelly Sandwiches—I get why they're capitalized, but Non-Hodgkin's Lymphoma? Stupid.

That began a one-year battle of fighting and healing and fighting and more healing. Some days way more fighting than healing. My journey of looking up started there.

Leah: As real life goes, Michele and I saw each other only in the parking lot of our girls' preschool. Have I mentioned that our oldest kids are girls and named Ava and are the same age? There was something real and cool happening between us in these short but daily parking-lot interactions. I remember the day, not the date, that Michele and I stood in that parking lot when I had one-year-old Ruby on my hip and her a bit more uncomfortable every day with baby Sam growing in her belly.

Michele was headed to Oklahoma City to visit her mom in the hospital. The way she said it caught my attention. I knew there was more to this story than a simple trip to the hospital. These phrases struck me: "non-Hodgkin's lymphoma ... cancer ... Momma is only fifty." Admittedly, I went to my most reliable research on lymphoma. Tell me everyone remembers Charlie from *Party of Five*. He had lymphoma, and he lived for many TV seasons. So based on that medical data, I wanted to be hopeful. There was something in Michele's face that worried me.

Weeks later and by total randomness, Michele and I ended up going on the same pumpkin-patch trip with our daughters. That day was much like our double date five months earlier; we had tons in common. My mom came along on that trip to help with my little, redheaded, one-year-old Ruby. A trip to the pumpkin patch with a one-year-old and a four-year-old is a two-man (I mean woman) job.

Michele: I met Leah's mom, Debbie, on that trip. I liked her very much, and she seemed to hook onto me immediately mostly because she was older and I was pregnant. That meant neither of us had to do anything we didn't want to, like going into the stinky petting zoo.

Debbie and I had plenty of time get to know each other. It was then that I started realizing everyone was taking extra precautions around Debbie and saying things like, "You look so good!" and "Leah, I can't believe your mom's here." And then Leah said, "Mom, don't forget you can't pick her up!" I could tell I was missing something.

Leah knew all about my mom, and just then, something was up with her mom. I mentally relived some of those parking-lot conversations. Nope, nope … she'd said nothing.

Leah: I remember exactly where I was standing on the pumpkin patch trip when Michele asked me, "Did something happen to your mom? What happened? I don't know anything." I admit I had been avoiding the topic for a month because it seemed unfair to put anything else on Michele. After all, we were barely friends and she was in a giant storm of her own.

To further my transparency here, I was still having trouble talking about what had been going on in my own family. On that fall day, though, my news was unavoidable.

I said, "On September 15, my mom had a heart attack at my house. It's been a long six weeks, but she's thankfully well on the road to recovery."

I was trying to be gentle and upbeat with the delivery of this information. The truth is that my life changed forever on September 15, 2011 at 3:15 p.m. My mom was young. She always had been. This lady has no quit in her. A power mom who had never needed sleep or downtime. I'd never seen anyone love motherhood the way she does. In my head, she'll always be thirty-six. I'm not sure why, but I have her stuck at that age.

But on September 15 … *Ugh!* My perfectly healthy, beautiful mom didn't just have a heart attack; it happened to her right in front of me. At my house. While we were chatting. In my kitchen. At my kitchen table. In my arms. Have you ever experienced anything like that? I hadn't. I didn't know it then, but my journey of looking up started there.

Michele: Did you see these dates? My tragedy and Leah's were exactly thirty days apart. With our moms! That still shocks me. Two girls who had met five months earlier and had wondered if they had anything in common found themselves standing in separate storms but facing each other. I had been standing in my storm by myself for sixty days. And then, Leah was hit by a similar storm. Was she whispering "Me too"?

Leah: There was this pull of a tragedy between Michele and me. We had sensed it but had no idea what was coming. The pull was deeper than a love for raw meat or Dolly Parton shows. I've learned that tragedies will always pull you toward something. Depression? Bitterness? Addiction? Denial? Jesus? A boob job? An unnatural urge for more spray tanning? There was this slow pulling on me. Something new was happening in me after what I saw happen to my mom. Something was happening for sure, and whatever it was, it was brand-stinkin' new. I was being pulled. Dragged. Whatever.

Michele: I'd say I was grasping for a straw or a life raft or maybe even just someone to listen. Mom's initial treatment didn't work, so we found ourselves at MD Anderson in Houston desperately seeking the help of the smartest or at least the best-marketed doctors in the United States.

Sleeping in a rollaway bed in the hospital room. Breast pumping in the bathroom. Hunting for dry ice to send my breast milk back to Oklahoma to my new baby. I woke up one morning at MD Anderson so heavy. I needed to take a walk. I gently started whispering a prayer to God not even really saying anything except "Help me." I heard a whisper. "Be thankful." Was that even possible at MD Anderson? Everywhere I looked, I saw images of cancer. Hairless people. IV poles. Yellow skin. But it wasn't just cancer. Everyone was barely moving as they walked through this hospital. So heavy. Slogging-through-wet-cement heavy. So many questions written on everyone's face. *Where are we sleeping tonight? What are we eating? What credit card should we use?* In that place, I could see marriages breaking down from all the stress.

How can I even begin to be thankful? How can I go back into that hospital room and tell my sweet momma to be thankful? My spirit heard more whispering about a positive spin on this circumstance. *What if I asked her about what her favorite thing about yesterday was? That might work.* Sometimes, the best thing that happened in a day was that it had ended. I know you've had days that you were just so happy to see end; bad news everywhere. But what if we focused on the good things? Could that change our perspective? Our lives? I wanted to take the next step from hearing that whisper to actually doing what it had told me to do.

Mom was a good sport and would always answer the question, "Mom, what was your favorite thing about today?" I don't remember all her answers, but one day she said, "Well, I didn't get diagnosed with cancer today." Now that's perspective-changing!

Leah: An ambulance came to my house and took my mom to the hospital. The ER doctor at Duncan Regional Hospital confirmed that my mom had had a heart attack. She was put on a helicopter and flown to Oklahoma City. Did you know that only the patient and the medical and flight team get to go on the helicopter? I swear I'd seen family members, especially terrified middle daughters, get on medical helicopters with their families on the TV show *ER*. I mean, I was needed in the middle of this medical emergency. If I didn't panic, who would?

7

Instead, my husband and I drove to the hospital in Oklahoma City to meet up with my dad. Once there, we heard she was already in surgery. The doctor told us what my mom had was unusual. "Highly unusual" were his words. She had no heart disease, so a stent would have been ineffective in her case. We were in the ominous wait-and-see group. *Great. Just great.*

They moved Mom to ICU, and we waited. And waited. Sometime during that night, my brother took a cell phone picture of me asleep in a chair at Mom's bedside, my fatigued body lying on her bed. In the picture, I can read the wall clock—4:22 a.m. Just over thirteen hours since everything had changed. There I sat. That picture alone tells the somberness of that night.

These things happen to people all the time. I'd been associated with the medical field day in and day out for nearly two decades by that point, so I knew these things happened. *But to my family? No way! To my mom?* I had greatly underestimated the toll a medical emergency could take on a family. My husband went back home that evening to take care of our babies. My dad, brother, and I stood around Mom's room for hours that night doing what her doctors said we had to do: wait and see.

I took cell phone pictures of my mom's monitor. Heart rate? Pulse? Oxygen level? Blood pressure? A billion other words I didn't even understand. I texted these pictures to my husband basically asking him to be her surgeon but still be ninety miles away with our kids. I kept asking if he saw a miracle coming or if he saw something else. Brutal.

Sometime in those late-night hours, I received a text message containing scripture from the Bible about faith and healing. I want to be transparent here. I'd been saved as a kid, and I was raised in church. I was so used to hearing Bible scripture from all kinds of people. I'll admit that scripture had never helped me before. Ever. I figured scripture was for people who were far less resourceful than I was. I didn't need scripture. I liked scripture just fine, but I didn't need it.

I was also not a fan of self-help quotes. I had my own brain, and I could crawl out of any ol' thing that happened. But sitting in that ICU room, you bet your butt I grabbed that scripture. I grabbed it and began to wrestle with it that night. I wanted help so badly. I was forced to make a choice, to take that next step of faith. *Do I believe or don't I? Is Jesus real or isn't He?* No middle ground. That's where I was. Feeling tension.

2

Rescued

Michele

Sickness. Frankly, I have a lot of experience with it. A lot. My mom was diagnosed with lupus and fibromyalgia when I was a freshman in high school, and I'm all too familiar with the ups and downs and the good days and the bad days of a person with a chronic illness.

I have a lifetime of experience in the world of sickness. I've woken up excited to do Black Friday shopping only to have it cancelled because it was a "bad" day. I've walked into a dark house full of depression more times than I can count. I don't like it. It's not my jam. Sickness is an enemy. It comes to steal, kill, and destroy. Where have I heard that before? It steals your experiences. It kills your joy. It destroys your relationships.

I didn't even believe her most of the time. Her not feeling well and needing to spend an entire day in bed. I didn't believe it. It's shameful to say, but it was true. What does it say about me that I didn't believe her? I never ever vocalized it. But this new thing was different. This was cancer. How can you argue with cancer? My mom's diagnosis of cancer changed my view, my perspective, and my relationship with her.

People who have sick family members focus on the tiniest details. They say things like, "Her white blood count came up two points today" and "She drank about a half cup of water two hours ago! I hope to get another half cup down her when she wakes up."

It's like if you try hard enough or learn enough about what the doctors are looking for, it will somehow translate to extra help for your sick family member. Help for her. I remember being insanely focused on her daily blood draws—every morning waiting for the report to come back, hoping and praying her white blood cell count would increase.

I wasn't raised in church, and I wasn't sure I had ever seen a prayer actually be answered. I would whisper desperate prayers for help, but I didn't think anyone heard me. I had a very hard time praying for complete healing because it was so exposing to my heart to pray for that. And if my prayer wasn't answered, what would that mean? If I prayed for healing and it didn't happen, would I question if God was real? What then? Is there hope without God?

Leah had started going to a Bible study in January 2012 and had invited me several times, but between running my own business, being a momma to a four-year-old and a newborn, being a wife, and driving back and forth to Houston every other weekend, I had little energy to tackle anything else. But I was ever so slightly seeking God, and Leah could see that. She would feed me scripture by way of text messaging, and it would be like drops of water on my tongue while trapped in the desert. It wasn't a lot of scripture—just enough to quench my thirst at the time.

Momma had been fighting for a long 350 days, and MD Anderson turned into hospice. Hospice. It was my turn to stay the night with Momma. Dad had stayed the night before, and I had gotten a good night's sleep. I convinced him to get some sleep and let me take that night. My aunt Donna had warned me not to stay the night because she was afraid Mom was going to die while I was there by myself. I scoffed at her boldness to expect my mom to stay by herself. I thought, *You don't even know! I've seen so much in this year. How dare you ask me to leave her? I'm not scared! How could I even think of myself when my mom's dying?*

This is something else that family members of sick people do. The more I can suffer, the better it will be on the patient, right?

The night was rough to say the least. Quite terrible actually, but Dad showed up at 7:00 a.m. to take me to breakfast. That was our thing. Momma would let Dad and me do breakfast or grab some coffee in the mornings. You read that right; she would "let" us.

I remember everything about that breakfast. Dad ordered his usual—pancakes and ham—and I had eggs and hash browns. We drank our coffee as if it were honey for our souls. Some businessmen were sitting directly behind me loudly discussing an all-important meeting they were about to attend as Dad and I were discussing funeral arrangements. Dad had made a list of possible pallbearers and was running them past me. I said, "Their stupid conversation sounds so insignificant and meaningless compared to ours." Dad shrugged and said, "Yeah. Don't I wish." They were sitting there in their pressed shirts tucked into their creased dress pants with shoes that matched their belts. *What do they know about a tough day?* We would have done anything to switch places with them. Anything.

We lost momma about an hour later. She passed away on August 1, 2012. We buried her on a Saturday, and my family and I went to church together the next day. That marked the first time we had stepped into church for church. We had been in churches lots of times but for funerals or weddings.

That same week, I attended Leah's Bible study, which she was then leading. That girl was sprinting straight to Jesus, and I wanted what she had.

As you can imagine, Leah and I experienced or were experiencing broken hearts at the same time. It's funny (not *ha ha* funny) to look back and see how our broken hearts left room for change. The old ways we had been living relying on our own strength were suddenly not working anymore. It was actually unavailable. We had been living with the notion that self-reliance was the best way to succeed. If people loved kittens or baby sea lions or needed support groups or had allergies or got the flu ever, that meant they were weak! You can see how this could be a breeding ground for a teeny-tiny amount of pride.

But what about when your formerly perfectly healthy mom is dying in your arms or from cancer? Then what? When you absolutely can't control your circumstances, where do you turn? She and I needed a new plan, a new strategy for life, and we were hungry for it. It was no accident that God walked us straight toward each other.

Between Bible study, church, and reading any book that might possibly help me understand this newfound love, I started to develop a kind of hunger I had never experienced before. I didn't know I could fall in love with Jesus, but I was doing just that. It was all I wanted to think and talk about. I started surrounding myself with people who were experiencing the same desire.

I began remembering certain people from my past who had a certain way about them, a light, a calmness, a contentment that seemed supernatural. I would seek their counsel and turn myself into a sponge when they would talk. I would soak in anything and everything they said. I wanted to tell anyone who would listen about this new relationship I was in. It's as if I had been introduced to a new buffet in town and it was the greatest thing ever! New foods, new flavors, new smells I had never experienced before. And the way I felt when I ate it? Man, I remember reading parts of the Bible and thinking, *Good gracious! I've wondered my whole life how to be a good friend, a good wife, and a good parent. Who knew the answers were in this book sitting on a shelf somewhere in my house collecting dust?*

I'm certain now that a lot of people already knew that. I told someone one time, "I felt as if I'd discovered John Piper and then I went to his website and realized he had written over a hundred books." Yep. Totally discovered him. You're welcome, John Piper.

My biggest fear was that it was too good to be true. *Is this just a fad? Is the bottom going to fall out? How am I living in this much peace? My mom just died! My fifty-one-year-old dad is living alone after thirty-five years of marriage! Come on! Please don't mistake this peace.*

But mine was not the fake peace you see on Sunday mornings. By peace, I don't mean that tears weren't falling. They were falling and falling often. There were days when I didn't want to get out of bed, but with me in that bed, I sensed a peace in the midst of my grief. The kind of peace that was superseding my circumstances.

Speaking of books, Leah received a copy of Bob Goff's *Love Does* at just the right time. She was moved by it. Touched by it. She urged me to stop reading whatever I was reading and start that book immediately.

I purchased it that day and downloaded it to my phone. That dude had my number. Everything in his book spoke straight to my heart. Mr. Goff wrote, "I used to think I could shape the circumstances around me, but now I know Jesus uses circumstances to shape me." *What? How can he articulate the exact feelings I'm experiencing? Is this a coincidence, or is there something more here?*

As I kept reading, I became more and more convinced that this was about more than a good author. It was about more than a coincidence. It was about something real and true. *Why did this book end up coming to me at that exact time in my life? Do I believe in God? Do I believe in Jesus? Do I believe He is listening? Do I believe in prayer?*

I do. And if I do, that has to change everything. I thought this was what a rescue looked like.

3

All In

Leah

When I was a freshman in high school living the dream of an Atoka Wampus Cat, I had a friend who was the most fun daredevil ever. Dare her to do anything and she would do it!

Someone once dared her to get a running start in our cafegymatorium and leap onto the stage, which was at least three feet high, maybe four. But she took that dare. She took off running, her face so determined like nobody's business. We watched as she took a flying leap and made it but not before scraping all the skin off her shin on the wooden stage. She wore that wound like a badge of honor.

Back then, I thought such risks were nuts. They were the furthest things from my plans. *Why would I do that? What if I got hurt? What if I didn't make it all the way onto the stage? What if I got in trouble? What was I supposed to be doing instead of such shenanigans?*

I thought she was bananas for having done something so

17

silly, but seeing her make it onto that stage ate at me. Jealousy is the formal name of what I was feeling. I was jealous that she had taken a risk and experienced something very cool because of it. The badge of honor I wore was the safety badge, the least sexy of all the badges.

My middle name is Gail, but a better middle name would have been Play It Safe Leah or Play It Safe Callicoat. Safe is always right in the middle of the crowd. Ol' Play It Safe never felt the need to stand out or to deviate from a prescribed plan. Safe was the equivalent of vanilla ice cream. Vanilla ice cream gets a bad rap. What's wrong with vanilla? It's the key ingredient in so many delicious desserts. And to kids with allergies, vanilla has never been accused of swelling someone's throat closed. Vanilla is the public service announcement of ice cream flavors. That's where I was. Vanilla. Never offensive. Never risky. Never leading a charge up a hill. Vanilla.

At age eight or nine, I purposefully made the decision to say yes to Jesus. I walked to the front of the church and told my pastor. My supportive parents stood with me as my pastor publicly shared my decision with the church. I did what the hymn we were singing was all about. I decided to follow Jesus. The pastor asked my parents and me to remain at the front of the church, and he encouraged the congregation to come up and shake our hands at the end of the service.

And I stood right there for nearly thirty years. I stood right there waiting. Waiting on heaven I suppose. In my defense, I thought that was what everyone who decided to follow Jesus was doing. I figured that my walking that church aisle was the most courageous thing Jesus would ever ask me to do.

Life was so vanilla. My type of vanilla went to church most Sundays wearing the right dress and Bible in hand, and thus nobody even noticed I was vanilla. Hello! Even I didn't know I was vanilla.

Years later, when I was in that dark ICU room with my sweet mom, who was fighting for her life, vanilla was totally useless. That text message I randomly received sitting in that ICU room contained this verse.

> Jesus turned and saw her. "Take heart, daughter," he said, "your faith has healed you." And the woman was healed at that moment. (Matthew 9:22 NIV)

I had no idea what to do with that passage, but I knew it was something new! That was the first time in my life that scripture had caught my attention. This scary situation with my precious mom was like a powerful tenderizer on my heart. God used this quiet moment to open my vanilla ears to hear Him for maybe the first time since that day nearly thirty years ago. I could hear Him! I knew I could hear about Him, but I didn't know I could actually hear Him with my own ears!

But that night in the ICU, I did. It was not an audible voice over the hospital intercom; it was that still, small voice I'd heard people talk about. I can tell you what that still, small voice told me. "Leah, don't you think it's weird that you say you believe in me but when your mom was dying in your arms, you said not one word to me?" I heard it so clearly. I heard those words deep in my being.

It turned out that I didn't feel I could trust someone I didn't know. I sure couldn't trust someone I didn't know with the things that mattered the most to me. I mean, my mom mattered big time to me! I didn't talk (pray) to God as my mom lay in my arms because I had no idea who He was or what He could do. I did, however, call 911 in haste. I knew for sure an ambulance would come to my house if I did. I called whom I knew for help. I couldn't pray because I had no idea how that worked or anything about the person hearing prayers.

That tension I mentioned earlier got very high right then, and that began changing me quickly. Soon, I was ready to answer the question, "Is He real or isn't He?" Sitting in my safe vanilla seat, I was sure to not see things any differently. But what if I moved? What if I said yes even once, even if it was a tiny yes? What could happen if I took the next step?

Three months after my mom got sick, I was invited to a Bible study. Being invited to a Bible study should not have been odd for a girl who was raised in church and was currently an adult in church. But hey, I'm just being real here—Bible study was not my jam. In my head, a ladies' bible study was all about casseroles, Bible drills, and denim dresses with kitty-cat appliqués. But I was on a treasure hunt as if my life depended on it. I didn't care where I started digging or who was watching as I dug. I knew that a treasure was to be found and that it had my name on it. All I had to do was find it; that still, small voice had told me so.

I said yes to my first Bible study on January 4, 2012. I didn't have a kitty-cat jumper, so I decided on jeans and a sweatshirt. Man, I hoped we would not be doing some weird foot-washing ceremony. I shaved my lower legs just in case. I grabbed my student Bible, a high school graduation gift from my parents dated 1993. It had my maiden name on it for heaven's sake. I had been married for nearly two decades! Thankfully, it still had that new-car smell.

Because my life depended on it, I was done being vanilla. Nowhere in the Bible was I called to be vanilla. In fact, the more I learned, the more I realized that being vanilla was a lot like being lukewarm. I believed for all those years that vanilla was safe and gentle and certainly not offensive. But in Revelation 3:15–16, Jesus vowed to spit such bland indifference out of his mouth. It turns out that being lukewarm sickens Jesus. When I read that, I was convicted. I knew without a doubt that He was talking about me. I was convicted to the point that I did an about-face repentance.

The Bible study I had been invited to was nothing like I'd feared. It included real girls sitting around a kitchen table every Wednesday at 8:00 p.m. searching to find out what God wanted His daughters to be about. Each week, we read the Bible and wrestled with what it said. We were not looking for us in the Bible but for Jesus. How many times in the Bible are we promised that we will find Him if we seek Him? Tons! We were seeking Him together every week, and guess what? I stinkin' found Him just as He had promised.

And He doesn't promise this only to me; He promises this to everyone! I'm no theologian, but even in the original Greek of the Bible, I think the word *everyone* means just that.

I sat around that table until the group got so big that we had to split up into smaller groups. I was asked to lead one of these smaller groups. I know, I know—I still didn't have a kitty-cat jumper, but I said yes anyway.

My group started meeting the same time every week. I held so tightly to this weekly meeting because the girls who came were seekers as well. It was like revival had hit. I poured my whole self into this treasure hunt, and guess whom I was still having parking-lot conversations with? Michele. In fact, our conversations were building the most beautiful friendship. My new friend was swimming as hard as she could every day. I had never seen anything like it. Her storm raged on and on, bigger and bigger every day. That was a strange, beautiful, and rare way to start a friendship—in times of crises.

We'd bonded initially over our moms being sick at the same time, but my mom made a full recovery and is alive and thriving. (And probably annoyed at my poking fun at kitty-cat jumpers. Sorry, mom!) Michele's momma continued to fight, and Michele continued to swim as hard as she could.

Michele's mom died in August 2012, and Michele joined my Bible study the next week. I remember the chair she sat in that night. It was big; she looked tiny in it. She had taken quite the beating during the previous year. The girls in my group had been consistently praying for Michele, so the first day she came was very emotional. She didn't have to tell her story; the others knew it. We'd been praying for her for so long.

Once I started reading what was in the Bible rather than waiting on a pastor to read it and spoon-feed it to me between

11:40 and 11:59 a.m. once a week, I began to understand whose I was. You won't believe what I found in the Bible. Hallmark cards ain't got nothin' on this book. (Warning: spoiler alert ahead.) The Bible told me that God was my defender, my friend, my counselor, my peace giver, and the lover of my soul. Holy cats! Even my 1993 student Bible would have told me that had I ever opened it.

Peace giver? Who has plenty of peace? Who would say, "I'm all set on peace. I'm full up"? I swear that anxiety is having its way with God's daughters, and I want all my sisters to know that we're not helpless against anxiety. Once you say yes to Jesus, you have the ultimate peace giver living in you; you just have to know how to engage Him. Guess what? If I'm running my life but I've asked Jesus to run my life, that will create anxiety in me. God has good plans for my life, but they are His plans.

> I know what I'm doing. I have it all planned out—plans to take care of you, not to abandon you, plans to give you the future you hope for. (Jeremiah 29:11 MSG)

So me being all in involved my surrendering the death grip I had on my life. I had to believe that the Holy Spirit was living in me and that He was given to me as a gift until I'm reunited with Jesus in my permanent home. And that meant I had to be all in. I had to push forward all the stuff I was working for years to protect and tell the dealer, "All in." And I had to mean it. All in could not be taken back. All in meant all in. I think that's true even in the original Greek. (Note to self: Get an English-to-Greek dictionary.)

4

Addicted to the Yes

Michele

In his book *Love Does*, Bob Goff described how love was a verb and we should all be doing it. Spreading love as Jesus did. He has a whole chapter dedicated to saying yes. I was officially inspired. I should be doing something! How could I believe in Jesus and not actually be following Him? Would I walk away from my fishing business as Peter did to follow Him? I had to start applying what I was learning to my real life. If Jesus were standing in front of me and asking me to follow Him, would I? What does that look like?

I decided to start praying for opportunities for Him to use me. I'd begin my days by saying, "Today is your day, God. Please have your way with me." I know what you're thinking—*Sure you did*. Listen. I had to start small. My first prayer went like this: "God, please help me remember to pray that prayer first thing in the morning."

I remember those mornings vividly. I'd sling my covers back and watch my feet move toward the carpet as I was uttering those words. He would remind me every morning before my feet would hit the ground. There was something about seeing my feet before I'd start my day that would remind me.

I have a friend who says, "This change is like a slow trickle." She's so right. Once I began asking Him to use me, the blinders started to slowly come off. In Acts 9, Paul talked about scales falling from his eyes and regaining his sight. I believe they are removed at a different pace for everyone because He knows you and me. Can you wrap your mind around that? What a concept. He knows me. He knows I'm a slow reader and can have a hard time with comprehension. Because He knows all this about me, He has the perfect prescription for my life. So we can forget about cookie-cutter religion. This is freedom. I like to think of it like snowflakes, each one being different but with the same snowflake Creator.

I said yes to Him on August 2, 2013, a year and a day after I'd lost Momma. Leah's neighbor had two extra tickets to a Christian women's conference, and to my surprise, I said yes to her offer of one. All I knew was that I wanted to get out of town.

I was nervous. I had never been to a women's conference before, and I didn't know the difference between Abraham and Moses. *What if someone finds out? What if someone sees my green Bible with my maiden name on it? Never mind. I won't even bring it. But what if someone notices I don't have a Bible? Eeek! I bet there's an app. Yay! There is indeed an app!*

I remember the speakers. I remember who the worship leaders were. It was the first time I had experienced the Holy Spirit jumping inside me as we worshipped. I raised my hands for first time at that conference. I experienced feelings and emotions and promptings I hadn't had before. I was falling in love with Jesus.

I ran up the stairs to go to the bathroom during one of the speakers hoping to go quickly with no line and grab some nachos. Leah and I have a hard-and-fast rule—if we're anywhere where those ballpark nachos are served, we absolutely have to eat them. Anywho, I was grabbing our nachos and a girl who was working the event stopped me. She was dressed in a navy-blue polo and khakis and had a broom and a dustpan in her hand. She asked, "How much were those?"

"These nachos?" I asked.

"Yeah."

I was immediately embarrassed. I didn't know. I'd just swiped my card. I'd been in a hurry because I wanted to get back to the speaker, and I knew they weren't $100, so I had just swiped and ran. I fumbled over every word I said to her and finally said while squinting to look at the menu that was at least fifty yards away, "I bet they're five bucks."

She said, "Don't worry about it. I'll look later."

I fumbled some more and asked, "Are you about to go on break?"

She said, "Yeah, my lunch break."

I responded without fumbling that time, "Oh! You want some nachos?"

She said, "No, I'll just eat at home."

Again, more fumbling. "Oh. You live close?"

She bit back, "No! I don't live close!"

Stars! *Take me out, coach!* I had jacked this up all kinds of ways. I could tell God wanted me to do something with her, but I didn't know what. I walked away in the most awkward way ever.

I got back down to Leah and tried to forget about my blunder. I spent the next ten minutes arguing with God. *What did you want me to do? I didn't have any cash. That's why I had to swipe my card for these nachos! I guess I could have given her my card and my PIN. Is that what you wanted?* Then *boom!* We were all released for a break.

Leah had to go to the restroom, so I waited for her outside. Y'all, guess what? The same girl walked in front of me twice. I heard that still, small voice say, *It isn't too late. Give her five bucks.*

Leah came out of the bathroom, and I basically attacked her. "Do you have a five?"

"Yes. Wait. Uh, I just have a twenty."

I was almost hysterical as I tried to explain what God had asked me to do. She got it. She proclaimed, "I'll find change. You find that girl."

I couldn't find her. I'd missed it. It was over. I'd just have to wait until the next time. Leah was bouncing from booth to booth asking for change, but no one would give it to her. I found Leah and told her to just stop. I'd given up. I no sooner got the words out of my mouth than the girl walked past me. I swiped the twenty out of Leah's hand and started to chase the girl. Sometimes for me, taking the next step involves a chase.

She was cutting through the crowd like a stinkin' hot knife through butter. *Good grief! How's she moving so fast? I can't keep up with her. Never mind. This is crazy. What would I say to her anyway? I can't do this. Too weird. Too much. I'm out.*

I turned around, and Leah caught my eye. It was evident that she would not let me give up in front of her. She was pumping her arm like Arsenio Hall and mouthing, *Go! Go!*

I exhaled deeply and said to God, "Hey! When I said use me, I meant to use me within my skill set and my comfort zone. I didn't ask for this!"

The girl slipped behind a black curtain where employees seemingly went to rest, and I followed her. I still remember my trembling hand reaching out to touch her shoulder before she went into what I assumed was a break room. She turned around. I was in it at that point.

I stuttered—but let's be honest; she was used to that from me by that point. I said, "Hi. Here." I placed the twenty into the pocket of her khakis.

She took a step back, almost offended. "Where did you get that? From your husband or something?"

Confused, I responded, "No, no. I just wanted you to have it and for you to know that I love you and Jesus loves you. I'm going to hug you now."

Her eyes filled with tears. I whispered in her ear as I hugged her, "Jesus loves you." I turned and walked back to Leah. I leaned against a cold, cement wall and slid to the ground. It was one of the toughest things I'd ever done. I was exhausted and so tearful from it.

Is this what following Jesus looks like? Chasing an employee of an event center through a crowd, stuffing money in her pocket, and then all that hugging? As crazy and nutty as it felt, I was addicted to the yes.

5

Some Yeses are Huge

Michele

God was pulling at my heart and creating a bigger hunger to want more of Him. A hunger to see more and say yes more. It wasn't a big, organized effort. It was simple. It was easy. It was then that people like Mother Teresa started making sense to my heart.

> *In this life, we cannot do great things. We can*
> *only do small things with great love.*
> —Mother Teresa

I'm not Mother Teresa, but her words removed the pressure that comes with the stigma of saying yes to God. Yes! I love this. See? This I can do. I can do small things right in front of me with great love.

Up until that point, I had thought that only headlining Christians were invited to do something with God. But then I realized that even I could *do something* with God. These two small words are giant. God is not an exclusive God. He is an inclusive God. Even you. Even me. Anyone who has ears to hear is invited.

The more I said yes to Him, the more I wanted to say yes again and again. I learned that saying yes to Him was more about being obedient than succeeding. That's because obedience *is* success.

Leah and I live in Duncan, in southwestern Oklahoma. It's home to about 23,000 folks. Duncan is the original headquarters of Halliburton, so you can imagine the industry in our area—oil and oil-related industries. And gas. And more oil.

Of course, since the 1980s, Duncan has worked very hard to diversify its industries to make the town and its people less dependent to oil and gas. Duncan is a town full of big-hearted folks who love to love. So full! But as with everywhere else on earth, there's a less-bright and less-sunny side to our community. It made world news in August 2013.

Like any small town, Duncan has its local paper with front-page news: a raging grass fire, a tornado, someone watering illegally during a three-year drought, and so on. But in the summer of 2013, the Duncan local news went worldwide.

Our rural Stephens County, only ninety-five miles southwest of Oklahoma City, had just experienced three heinous, senseless crimes resulting in three deaths in less than a year. Braylee Henry, a sixteen-year-old girl, was murdered in a convenience store by a young man in the summer of 2012. Alyssa Wiles, a fourteen-year-old girl who loved to dance, was stabbed to death by her teenage boyfriend in early June 2013. Then in August 2013, three teenage boys drove passed Chris Lane, an athlete from Australia, while he was jogging, and gunned him down. All these crimes were senseless and vicious. Hearts all over our county were breaking, and fear was running rampant. These crimes had something horrifying in common—they had been committed by young people ranging in age from fifteen to twenty-one.

There was so much statewide media coverage regarding the murders of those precious young girls, and the outrage and horror of Chris Lane's murder was on a worldwide scale, like nothing Duncan had ever experienced. Our town of 23,000 was invaded by reporters from all major networks such as CNN, Fox, and CBS. And that was just the American press covering the story. The media in Australia (the *West Australian*, the *Sydney Morning Herald*, etc.) was covering the tragedy as much as the American media was. Duncan was under fire for being the hometown of such vicious murders.

I saw a national news story that showed the makeshift memorial marking the location of Chris Lane's murder. The cameraman zoomed in on one of the many posters at the memorial site. This poster was a beautiful picture of Chris Lane in his baseball uniform and it read, "Duncan calls their kids the DUNCAN DEMONS. This is the man they killed."

So many emotions and a lot of bad publicity were being pumped into Duncan. Everyone was heartbroken and nervous. The only other time I had experienced a feeling like that was on September 11, 2001. We all just felt so helpless and powerless and destructible. Our small, safe Oklahoma town had been rocked; frankly, we were being attacked. It was as if the rocks in Duncan were crying out for help.

So many questions. How did this happen? Will this happen

again? What was going on in the minds of these young men? Did they not value human life? Did they not value their own lives? Did they understand that their community cared about them? Did they know they had potential? Did they know their decisions, good and bad, would affect people in their community? Can we do something? What can we do?

I had just learned I was supposed to be doing something. I had just confessed to God fourteen days earlier, "Use me!" Did I mean what I said? You bet your butt I did.

School started that year on August 20th, and everyone was trying to move forward with a regular life. You know that feeling; it can feel a bit desperate seeking normalcy after something so tragic has happened. It's as if we fight for normalcy to try to Band-Aid the pain. The first day of school went perfectly, and our two Avas were officially first graders.

Later that night, all Duncan Public School parents received a message stating that there had been a threat against the high school. Because of it, all Duncan schools would be on lockdown the next day. Parents had to make a decision—either risk sending their children to school or keep them home. The school was not going to count any child absent.

The next day was not just the second day of school; it was Ava Miller's sixth birthday. We decided to take the Avas to school, and in keeping true to our roots, Leah and I were in deep discussion in the parking lot after the drop-off. Leah had planned to take a special lunch to eat with Ava in the cafeteria and drop off cupcakes for Ava to share with her class. The lockdown had Leah wondering if she would be allowed into the school for the celebration.

It hit me just like that. Ava Miller might have to miss her celebration at school that day, but while that was sad, we knew she would be celebrated at home. But what about other kids who didn't have birthday celebrations at home or school? What about the kids who just needed that extra something on their birthdays? I wondered if this was the it we had been searching for.

I asked Leah, "What if we could celebrate the birthdays of every kid in the Duncan Elementary School system?" Those sixteen words started something wonderful. We probably could not have done anything to prevent those terrible crimes ten minutes before they were committed, but what if we had done something ten years earlier? What if we purposefully connected our community to our young students and told them face-to-face that they mattered?

We decided Leah should pay attention to and celebrate her Ava but also look at the other kids in the cafeteria and note their reactions to Ava's celebration. Leah was able to get into the school, and she called me afterward. She said, "Dude, I think you're onto something."

This is it.

I emailed Dr. Sherry Labyer, our school district's superintendent; my subject line read, "Possible Birthday Program: You do not have to read this." It's not that I didn't want her to read it; I just wanted to make it clear that I recognized the pressure she must have been under given the recent events. The three boys charged with Chris Lane's murder were students in her school system. I wrote that Leah and I had an idea we wanted to pitch but were happy to talk about it later. To my surprise, she invited us to her office the next day.

Leah and I walked into the superintendent's office with shaky knees. I think we had something printed on paper, but I can't tell you what it was. I just remember the paper shaking in my hands. I started to back out. *Why would she meet with us? What if she says no? Is this a silly idea? What did we know about helping kids?*

But we sat in her office and poured our hearts out. We told her that we were committed to gathering and organizing members of our community to help our young people on the heels of these tragedies by celebrating kids' birthdays.

She loved it! She said, "Go! I want you to go to Woodrow Wilson Elementary, and I want you to celebrate the fourth and fifth graders as a pilot. Those babies will be gone to middle school next year." Woodrow Wilson is a Title I school with the highest percentage of students who receive free or reduced lunches in Duncan.

Beautiful Day Foundation was born that second. This little newborn could not even hold its head up, but what it lacked in experience and muscles, it made up for with passion. We received that yes from our passionate and rock star of a superintendent on August 22, and we planned our first party for August 30, 2013. Warp speed!

We celebrated 107 children's birthdays that first year—107! That was gigantic! A hundred and seven kids heard the message— The day you were born was a Beautiful Day! They heard this message face-to-face from people in their community, people from different neighborhoods and all sides of town.

A Duncan community member once aggressively asked us if we really thought a birthday celebration at school would make any difference in anyone's life and in our town. Umm … We had no idea. But doing nothing wasn't an option for us.

I thought about Mother Teresa's quote about doing small things with great love. These birthday celebrations fit that perfectly. So simple. So pure. Nothing complicated.

Saying yes was where we were, and this yes was huge. And yeses that huge don't happen easily. A gigantic and special thanks goes to the fabulous superintendent Dr. Sherry Labyer and Woodrow Wilson's warm-hearted principal Lisha Elroy.

6

Love Gets Legs and Stain Sticks

Leah

So there we were really doing this thing. Taking the next step. And the next.

Celebrating the birthdays of these precious kids at Woodrow Wilson Elementary had created a passion in me. Spreading the message "The day you were born was a Beautiful Day" was a calling from that still, small voice. It was so clear. My bones could feel it. You know those moments where your love goes from feeling to action? There it was—love growing legs in that cafeteria month after month.

Michele and I needed an army to help us, so we did what girls do—we grabbed our best girlfriends and even some new friends. Telise (pronounced *Ta lease* as in Ta rent, Ta own, Ta lease). Melissa. Cheryl. Krista. These are not ordinary friends; they are steroid friends, friends with no quit in them. Friends who love saying yes. Friends who always have a glue gun or bejeweled hammer in their cars.

These friends grabbed their people. And those people grabbed their people. Before we knew it, we had a posse of fifty real, live people in our community who wanted to walk this same love into the Woodrow Wilson cafeteria.

We all felt compelled to be there. The more kids we met and the more stories we heard from these kids, the more we couldn't stay away. One party was not enough. Two parties were not enough. Rose, a fifth-grade girl with a peaceful countenance, told us one month about her momma being pregnant. Rose was already caring for a smaller sibling during the night, and it was startling to see the excitement on Rose's face about the new responsibility coming her way. The next month, Rose shared that her mom had lost the baby. She was heartbroken. But we were there to hear this story and help shoulder a tiny bit of her burden.

Fixing people's problems can be overrated. Sitting face-to-face with others, just listening to them and being available, not looking away when a broken heart is so visible—that's where we were.

Here's what we found. So many people want to help; they want to do life with purpose. My life was crying out to be busy for a purpose. My head hitting the pillow exhausted each night after being busy all day wasn't enough to give my life meaning, and I knew it.

It turns out that I'm not alone in that. Our pool of Beautiful Day volunteers was as diverse at those little faces in the cafeteria. God knows what He's doing. People were saying yes to join us, but we knew they were not saying yes to us. God's calling has a sweetness to it.

The Woodrow Wilson principal told us that the kids in her

school came to school first to be loved, second to eat, and third to learn. This was so hard to hear, but Michele and I feared it was a sad truth.

Let me tell you about one of our Woodrow Wilson Beautiful Day volunteers, Miss Cathy. She is a woman who understands firsthand what the principal had told us. Cathy's son had gone to Woodrow Wilson years ago, and back then, Cathy was a different person. Today, she's a confident, loving, gorgeous, energetic, joyful woman. People are drawn to Cathy because of her funky-colored hair and her art gallery of tattoos, but her real magnet is her heart. She's never met a stranger; her love doesn't have to be earned. She's real everywhere she goes.

Cathy shared with us that when her son was a student in this elementary school, she was not whom we see now. Back then, she was struggling terribly with her role and her responsibilities as his mom. Back then, her life was full of things that it's no longer full of, things that left scars on her, things she has since been fully and totally freed from.

She told Michele and me, "I sure needed some help when my son went to school here. I needed someone to come along beside me and fill in for my son's sake. If only something like Beautiful Day would have existed back then ... So that's why I'm here. I'm a different person today, and now I can help come alongside a mom who maybe finds herself where I was. I can help celebrate her child."

To know Cathy's story makes her involvement in Beautiful Day even more precious. Cathy inspires people around her every day. She inspires us to use our stories to free people from bondage into the life God created for them.

A few months had gone by, and Michele, our army, and I were celebrating birthdays in that cafeteria. We had experienced and worked out so many kinks by that point. Usually the hard way. Remember the month I showed up with all passion but no birthday cards, no birthday bracelets, no birthday tablecloth, and no balloons? Yeah. Me neither. Thank you, Jesus, for giving me mercy when I drove like Danica Patrick back to my house to get these things. #driving75inaschoolzone #Godsmercy.

Every month, Beautiful Day volunteers go into elementary schools and celebrate every child who has a birthday that month. We decorate some of the lunchroom tables to look like a birthday party complete with party plates, tablecloths, and balloons. At each place setting is a special meal, a Beautiful Day bracelet, and a custom-made birthday card telling the children with birthdays, "The day you were born was a Beautiful Day."

And here's the most important part of the party setup: there's an empty seat between these special birthday place settings. Beautiful Day volunteers sit in those seats so they can engage face-to-face with the birthday kids. These twenty-minute birthday parties are twenty-minute connections. They're everything. Right there at the lunch table, kids realize they are seen and valued and poured into and heard. This extends to all kids, even kids who are well loved in their homes. Being seen by your community is a universal craving regardless of socioeconomic, nationality, race, or religious differences. If you haven't had lunch with a fourth grader in an elementary school cafeteria, Michele and I highly recommend it.

By November, the birthday program was running smoothly. We had plenty of volunteers and even some donors. We were having a blast and were totally comfortable. We were loving getting to know the 300-plus kids in that school. One of the best lessons we learned that first year was more of a best practice—we learned that stain sticks or stain remover were a must-have for our volunteers. When elementary school kids hug, they hug with their whole bodies, pizza sauce–covered cheeks and all, but tomato sauce ain't got nothin' on our stain sticks.

We all wear white Beautiful Day T-shirts to the parties. A kid once told us, "You guys are all dressed alike. You look like servants." Right on, kid.

We learned another much harder lesson after only two months of celebrations. We encourage our volunteers to interact with the kids in an organic way—no agendas. Kids can smell a fake a mile away, so it's important that our volunteers feel free to be themselves so the kids will respond with that same honesty.

After two birthday parties, Michele and I created our only rule for our volunteers in regard to what they can say to the kids. Do not ask the kids what they did or what they got for their birthdays. This is such an innocent, normal question to ask, right? But I asked a fourth-grader that question, and he answered with another question: "What do you mean? I'm doing it right now. My mom says she doesn't have the money for me to have a party this year." Big sigh. I will always wish I could have stain-sticked my question out of that conversation.

7

Irish Twins

Leah

Irish twins: A pair of siblings born less than 12 months apart, especially if born within the same calendar year.

If the birthday program was Beautiful Day's firstborn, we were soon to experience the joy and panicked exhilaration of having Irish twins.

I need to tell you about the shower in my bathroom. It's not just a shower. That small tiled room is like church for me, and in there, Jesus and I have had so many conversations. One day, I fear He's gonna ask me to scrub the grout in the corner of this church. Until then, I'll ignore that holy mold.

In late fall of 2013, I was minding my own business and taking a shower when Jesus spoke to me. He had never spoken this particular word to me before. "Widows." It happened exactly like that. Years ago, my Grannie lost my Papa and my Nana lost my Granddaddy, and I mourned those losses terribly. They were

45

amazing men! But mourning those losses as a granddaughter and aching for my grandmothers were as far as my passion to *serve* widows went. I know. *Ugh!* You're welcome, Jesus.

After I heard that word, I hopped out of the shower and immediately called Michele. I told her what God had just said. Silence. We just sat there for a minute. We both love to say yes, but we didn't know the question, so neither of us said anything. We agreed to just put it on the shelf. After all, we had just barely gotten the birthday program going. In those past few months, we had formed a Beautiful Day Foundation Board (with bylaws, Articles of Incorporation, budgets, financials, R2D2s, and other complex words). We should mention here how every board needs "a Cheryl". Our Cheryl has an amazing capacity for loving people really well and also has the super powers of budget management, spreadsheets and organization! If you don't have "a Cheryl", you need one! How in the world would we explain to our new board that our mission was loving on elementary age kiddos but that this new idea was also our mission too? I couldn't see how, so Michele and I just stayed quiet about it.

We've all been there—shelving those things we don't understand yet. What's the difference between dragging my feet and shelving something? Or the difference between not taking the next step and disobeying God? Good questions. Send me an email if you know the answers. It was brutal thinking about starting something new when we were currently in the very early stages of this other new thing. But Michele and I sure do love saying yes. We love it. (Our favorite meme: "That's a horrible idea. What time?") Yes to all things crazy and cool and fun and wild especially if eating sour cream and cheddar Ruffles is part of the planning process.

Michele and I have a unique leadership style. Once, Che told us he felt we had a Marmaduke leadership style. I know, I know. You won't read much about this style in top-selling leadership books. At least not yet. But Che said multiple times that he had witnessed Michele and me rushing into a room overflowing with good intentions and energy and passion. Never lacking passion. Or fire. That we'd burst into the room rip-roaring and ready to go. Running fast.

For those of you who have no Marmaduke reference, how about the movie *Marley and Me*? In so many scenes, Marley's running wild, tipping over lamps and clearing coffee tables with his whipping tail. I suppose Michele and I have a style that resembles that—passionate and crazy energetic. Once in a board meeting, Michele found herself in one of these whipping-tail moments, and as she talked about a difficult phone call one of us needed to make, she was passionately telling the board what she would say on that call. Her tail knocked lots of stuff off the coffee table and onto the floor. Our sweet friend Telise said, "Or … or … or maybe *I* could make the phone call for you." If you identify with this leadership style, we recommend you find yourself a Telise. She's our official filter.

Michele and I read Bill Hybel's phenomenal *Courageous Leadership* book. He did not mention the Marmaduke style, but he did write about different spiritual pathways Jesus followers take that lead them into a room in which they feel particularly close to God. He wrote that there were a number of different pathways and they were all sacred. There was one in particular that rang true for both of us: the activist pathway.

> They're happiest when white knuckled and gasping for breath. Because of their wiring they need – actually they revel in – a highly challenging environment that pushes them to the absolute edge of their potential. It's when they're right on that edge that they feel closest to God …

> Scores of such men and women received a calling from God, burst out of the starting blocks, and ran full speed from the day they received their orders until the day they keeled over and died.

That describes us exactly.

Some of our friends used to get together to pray over a Bible study I lead. Every Wednesday morning, we'd gather and pray. Just pray. No plotting, planning, or list making. Only sitting still and praying together. Do you know how hard that is for a pack of gals? One Wednesday morning just a few months after "Widows" was whispered in my shower, our friend Jan asked for some prayer before we began. She had gotten a very clear message from God the Sunday before, and she wanted us to pray over her as she began unwrapping what He had said to her.

She had been sitting behind four widows in her church that previous Sunday morning and had heard clearly from God that she was supposed to be ministering to widows. Some way. Somehow. Keep in mind that only Michele and I (and our husbands—those poor dudes probably wish we would keep something—anything—to ourselves) knew what God had said to me in my shower months earlier.

Immediately, I unshelved what I had heard from Him. Right then and there on the floor of my living room, something new was born for Beautiful Day. Right then, Michele and I knew without a doubt that God was calling us to serve widows in some way, and He had sent Jan to help us. Jan of all people! She is one of the amazing women in our lives that we (accidentally) bullied into mentoring us.

Jan is also steroid friend, a professional, a powerful female leader in her church and her family. She's been walking closely with the Lord for decades. She was already a mentor to me and to so many others. I'll never forget that moment. God kept helping us build the coolest army in all the land.

We were still not sure exactly what to do with this whisper. A monthly lunch? A monthly dinner? A community garden? A newsletter? A kickboxing class? We knew we were moving forward on this new serving opportunity, but we had no real direction. So we sat and waited.

One Saturday, my family and I went for lunch at a local restaurant. When we went in, I noticed two women seated at a table near the front. They were beautiful older women chatting and eating together. Something about them caught my eye. I have no idea what, but I was fully aware of their presence the entire meal. They were finishing up at the same time we were, so we kind of just bumped into each other leaving the restaurant. One of the women knew my husband and wanted to meet our kids. I made small talk with the other woman. I said, "How nice for you gals to get together to share a meal. Are you celebrating something special?"

This nice woman answered, "No, not really. We both lost our husbands this year, and we like to get together for lunch or dinner often. We sure have a lot in common and a lot to talk about."

As soon as I got to my car, I was overwhelmed with the clarity of God's calling for us to minister to widows. I called Michele and bawled into the phone, "That's it! God's being crystal clear. We *must* do this. We must take the next step. Soon! I'm certain He's telling us this!"

Thankfully, Michele could understand my blubbering. She was a yes. An easy yes. Just as always. Again, God's calling had a sweetness to it.

Soon after that day, we formed Kindred Community, an initiative of the Beautiful Day Foundation. We decided on a monthly evening event for women in our community who had lost their husbands. Thanks to our board member and also talented decorator, Melissa, these events would look much like fancy wedding receptions complete with gorgeous meals served on real dishes, centerpieces you hope you'd get to take home, and informational or inspirational programs. Beautiful Day volunteers would wear aprons when serving these specials guests and taking care of any need they saw.

The first dinner was held on September 16, 2014; forty-nine brave ladies came to this new gathering. Michele walked one woman to her car that night and was told, "Hey, I want you to know there are more of us. Most of us here tonight are scouts."

After that first dinner, we cleaned up the dining area and took out the trash. Some of us dragged our dog-tired bodies back to my house for a debriefing. Have you ever attended a debriefing immediately following a calling coming alive? It's weird. In a typical debriefing, voices are loud, excited, and almost cackling as people share stories. But that debriefing was different. We sat quietly and in awe all over my kitchen practically whispering the things each of us had seen. We all spoke in half sentences, half thoughts.

"That lady in the blue scarf …"

"I never expected to see …"

"She told me there are more …"

"All those volunteers? Where? How?"

This debriefing was almost reverent. We figure this must be what it feels like to taste and see His goodness. One dinner was not enough.

By our second anniversary, 230 widows were joining us at these monthly dinners, and the number is growing. These women walk into a room full of other women who truly understand how they feel and the season they're in. And the voices in the room are those of women whispering, "Me too."

It turns out that having Irish twins is very cool, crazy, and amazing. And yes, they're both still in diapers.

They Just Keep Coming

Michele

When we jumped in, there was so much we didn't know, but we knew we had to take the next step to see more. We didn't know if the kids would like the parties. We didn't know if the principals would feel that we'd joined their mission. We didn't know if the widows would be looking for a safe place to gather.

And we didn't know that people were looking for a place to serve. One of our volunteers who had been with us for about six months told us, "I've been in Duncan for nearly thirty years, and I've never felt I belonged to a group. The Kindred Community volunteers make me feel I belong here." That's hard to hear. It still surprises me that people can feel alone in a town of 23,000.

We did know from the first day in that Woodrow Wilson Elementary cafeteria that it was right where God wanted us to be. How did we know? Once we said yes to His calling, He kept sending us people who would say yes to us.

Superintendent: yes

53

Principal: yes.

Volunteers: yes.

Donors: yes.

Very early on, we knew we needed to continue to learn, and thankfully with every yes, we did learn. We knew that if we just kept our eyes open, He would show us what He wanted us to see and what we needed to see. It was then that I started to feel like the disciples in the gospel who were just too sleepy to pray for our Savior. I knew He wanted to show me some cool stuff, but it was so easy to get tied up in the details of everything that needed to be done to complete the task.

But what if I kept my eyes open while doing the tasks? If I didn't fall in love with the tasks but with the calling, what would I see? What would I learn?

I learned to turn myself into a sponge and soak up everything in the room. *What can I learn here? Is there an opportunity for me to love on someone right here? Where? Show me. Show us.*

> Ask me and I will tell you remarkable secrets you do not know about things to come. (Jeremiah 33:3 NLT)

Seeing people. Really seeing people. Learning how to love people just by listening, smiling, hugging, and serving. It turns out that the best way to love on others is to serve alongside them. You always hear the analogy about people trying to put a cart together while running downhill. At Beautiful Day, it seems our cart is rolling uphill because it's harder, but we like hard things. One of our founding members coined the phrase, "We walk toward the hard things." With her fancy handwriting, Telise penned this on Christmas gifts for our team. This saying is a treasure!

Building a relationship with someone while you're running uphill and putting a cart together makes for the fastest-building relationships in all the land. When your wheel falls off and someone you just met picks it up and puts it back on, that means something special. Trust is built immediately, and the helper feels needed immediately. I want to be a part of a team of people who want to do something for the kingdom.

A wheel fell off one October at a Beautiful Day party at Woodrow Wilson Elementary. A first-grade boy came to the birthday table hesitant but thankfully not hesitant enough not to take a seat. His teacher told us he was a new student and spoke only Spanish. Learning Spanish is on my bucket list, but the shrink-wrap is still on my Rosetta Stone. I'm gonna learn Spanish. I will. Someday. ¿Donde esta mi Rosetta Stone?

But that day, my desire to learn Spanish was helping me none. Wheel off! What do we do? Do we just sit and stare at this kid as our English gets louder and louder hoping he understands something?

Finally, an amazing volunteer remembered a third grader we had celebrated just the month before who spoke Spanish and English! He was in the cafeteria, so she went and grabbed him, gave him a slice of pizza, and sat him beside our new friend. I know all the rule-followers out there are thinking, *But he's not a birthday kid. He can't have pizza. He already had his turn!* But this third grader became a volunteer that day. He sat there away from his friends the entire lunch period and translated for us. He didn't know this kid, but he knew what he had experienced the month before, and he was willing to be a bridge for Beautiful Day to communicate with this birthday boy. Wheel on!

Have you ever seen a closed door with a sign that read Do Not Open or Employees Only and your desire to open it was so overwhelming that you just had to see what was inside?. God was inviting us to open that door. He was calling us to see more. He invited us to be dragged on this journey of discovery to find out more about ourselves and more about Him.

So they come. They join us. People are drawn to this. They want to be a part of it. When we human beings experience this kind of love, we want to share it with our friends. So what do we do? We invite them to serve alongside this diverse group of people who want to see behind that door.

When I was little, I thought once you got your life "right" with God, everything would fall into place. Oh who was I kidding? I thought this a few years ago. I would look at these women with these beautiful, put-together families who went to church every week and think, *Man. They're doing it right. No problems.* Can I be straight with y'all? I wasn't drawn to that. Even as a kid. It intimidated me, and it made me feel hopeless. I remember thinking, *I'll never be put together like that. Never.* The truth is, I won't ever be right with God, not on this side of heaven. He can look at me only because of Jesus. Realizing this truth for the first time as an adult was so freeing. He loves me anyway. He loves me before I put on my makeup and perfume. He loves me before

I step foot in church or join a Bible study or become a church member or do anything for Him. He simply loves me.

This is the kind of love Jesus wants us to share with our neighbors. It's in the Bible, yo.

When we started Kindred Community, we knew we were right where God wanted us to be. Friends, 49 beautiful souls showed up on our first night. We had 20 volunteers serve in a genuine way. That was September 2014. By that time, we were in two elementary schools celebrating 504 children, and we had about 120 volunteers saying yes to the same calling we had.

By fall 2016, we had eight elementary schools in four school districts signed up to be Beautiful Day chapters and had celebrated almost 2,500 children. By fall 2017, we had twelve elementary schools in eight school districts signed up to be Beautiful Day chapters and celebrating nearly 4,000 kiddos! There are more schools interested; they're on our wait list.

Kindred Community events were averaging 230 ladies attending intimate dinner parties monthly, and the volunteers. And they're still coming. It's beyond thrilling to carry such missions forward with all kinds of people!

The numbers don't lie. I know, I know … numbers, snumbers, blumbers, zumbers, and cucumbers. I know there is a lot of controversy in ministry over the obsession with numbers. The higher numbers you report, the closer you are to God, right? Wrong. The gospel is about the one right in front of you. The heart that is changing right in front of you. The man in the mirror. Ol' Michael Jackson was onto something. My soul tells me that numbers *are* important. And one is indeed a number. I said from the first day in that elementary parking lot, "If the only heart that is changed is my heart, is that enough? What if my daughter's heart was the only heart changed? Enough?" You bet your butt it's enough. A changed heart for God changes another heart and another heart and the next one and the next one and the next one. Wait. Have I heard that before?

> Therefore, go and make disciples of all nations, baptizing them in the name of the Holy Spirit. (Matthew 28:19 NLT)

> This is good and pleases God our Savior, who wants everyone to be saved and to understand the truth. (1 Timothy 2:3–4 NLT)

Everyone sounds like a big, giant number. The harvest is ready but the workers are few (Matthew 9:37). We are answering a call, and He needs workers.

We have a mentor who has a prayer, "God, please send me what I need to serve those you send." We have stolen this prayer, and we see it answered every day.

They just keep coming. Thank you, Jesus, for being so faithful.

In the beginning, we didn't know we were forming a nonprofit and sure didn't know we needed a checking account. There was no big, elaborate plan to create any financial statements out of this. We used a gallon ziplock bag kept safely in Leah's car console for the first few months of Beautiful Day's life. In our classy plastic safe were some coins and a few dollars and some receipts. Nothing ever happens until it does for the first time. And one day it did.

We were blessed with a real live donor. A hundred bucks in cash. It was given to Leah through a drive-thru window at a flower shop. Our precious friend Jacklyn is a local business owner and had seen us with our clear plastic bag and, right then gave us a $100 bill and a real bank bag! She later became our first corporate partner! *Woo hoo!* We'd just gotten called up to the big leagues!

Volunteers keep coming. Thank you, Jesus. Donors keep coming. Thank you, Jesus. People have heard of this Beautiful Day story and felt the pull to give in generous ways to allow us to continue celebrating children and impacting widows. Thank you, Jesus. We don't know exactly who all of this is for. We really don't. Our friend who handed Leah that $100 through a drive-thru window felt something for Beautiful Day that required a response from her. Her feeling turned into action. Her love grew legs. Doesn't love do that? Doesn't love prompt outward expressions of internal stirrings? We don't know a whole lot, but what we know is rooted in truth. God's truth.

Love is contagious. The spirit of service is contagious. In our communities, we are all much more alike than different. Those serving and those served want the same things—to see others and to be seen. Thanks to two of our board members, Corey Ensey and Kimber Budowsky, our fundraising and marketing style is now powerfully purposeful and driven to not just raise funds but also to firmly establish our communities as stakeholders in the impacts of Beautiful Day.

Contagious behavior doesn't happen just between adults. What about your kids watching you? A billion studies have proven that children watch their parents carefully and mimic what they see. Yikes. That's some pressure for you. If nothing else, Leah's and my kids and our board members' kids have seen their parents giving away a whole bunch of free love. We hope this spirit of service infects our kids.

9

Gas, Water, and Salt

Michele

The rest of this book is dedicated to the beautiful lessons we've learned while putting the cart together and rolling it uphill and while taking care of two precious Irish twin babies who are still in diapers.

Misery loves company. I hear this, and sadly, it rings true to me. I have always had a lot of girlfriends, and some of them were friends because we had the same things to grumble about. Isn't that interesting? I've had full-blown "friendships" built on a foundation of bitterness, hatred, and jealousy and then wondered why I left a party feeling those "friends" were now talking about me.

When you start a relationship with someone based on nasty talk whether it be regular gossip, church version of gossip that some try to disguise as prayer requests, jealousy over the same person, hatred, or bitterness, it is dark and sad. There is no light or joy there. To my surprise, that kind of relationship usually ends the same way it started—with gossip, jealousy, hatred, and bitterness.

Ol' mother gossip loves a party. One of the hardest things I'm learning to overcome as a believer is talking about God's children. The truth is, I still struggle with it.

> The tongue runs wild, a wanton [needless] killer. With our tongues we bless God our Father; with the same tongues we curse the very men and women he made in his image. Curses and blessings out of the same mouth! (James 3:7–10 MSG)

What? We curse the women who were made in His image? With the same tongues we sing His praises? That hurts my feelings.

Before I was a believer, I would hear Christians say things that made absolutely no sense to me. That would turn me off in a heartbeat. If I had heard someone say, "You have tools to combat this problem," I would have cast that off as if it were nonsense and gone looking for some *real* help.

Leah and I have an analogy we use all the time: "Do you want water or gasoline?"

We look at our problems in this life as tiny fires and sometimes gigantic fires. As girlfriends, we have the choice to douse these fires with gasoline or water.

When you throw gasoline on a fire, what happens? Yep. An explosion. That's what I'm talking about. A friend of mine comes to a girls' night frustrated with her man because he didn't put the recycling out on recycling day. Yes, while that's frustrating, it's hardly grounds for a divorce or even continued anger. Gasoline is just that—gasoline. It magnifies the problem. It makes it worse. You might think you're helping by joining the fight, but in actuality, you're just turning the tiny flame into a firestorm. The gasoline feels like so much fun at the time, but the sweetness and pureness of water always lets you see the truth of the situation. Water doesn't distort the circumstances; it makes them clearer.

So what does this water look like? Water is a lot of listening and some more listening and then more listening. No judgment. Just listening. Most of the time, water is just not gasoline. Sometimes, water is reminding your friends of the truths they want to be reminded of. Water washes off all the impurities the world tells us we are justified in thinking. Sometimes when you are giving water, it will lead you straight to your saltshaker, salt being the truth.

This is the sweet spot. When you sit back and listen, it's much easier to hear God. He will guide you through guiding your friend. It was not a coincidence that Jesus referred to Himself as the Living Water. Water given by a true friend poured on a real problem is like a thirst quenched after being on the lake all day.

While misery loves company, the same thing is true at the opposite end of the spectrum. Love is contagious. Kindness is catching. Serving people is infectious.

People are passionate. We were all made to love and be relational. We all have to decide what that love, kindness, and spirit of service look like. For a long time in my life, showing love looked like a gallon of gasoline, a bunch of matches, and maybe some brass knuckles. I honestly thought I was helping my girlfriends when I'd jump in on the fight. I didn't know there was another way to love my friends and neighbors.

All this is true and even with Beautiful Day. Our behavior and attitude is contagious. Good and bad. In his book *Love Does*, Bob Goff wrote, "Love like you are made of the stuff." We are loving people like we're made out of love. This love has been given to us freely, and we were giving it away in the same way we received it—for free!

We quickly realized that while we had been called to two particular groups of people—children and widows—our mission did not stop there. Leah and I knew we couldn't expect our volunteers to pour out love when they hadn't experienced it themselves.

> Let me tell you why you are here. You're here to
> be salt-seasoning that brings out the God-flavors
> of this earth. If you lose your saltiness, how will
> people taste godliness? You've lost your usefulness
> and will end up in the garbage. Here's another
> way to put it: You're here to be light, bringing out
> the God-colors in the world. God is not a secret
> to be kept. We're going public with this, as public
> as a city on a hill. If I make you light-bearers, you
> don't think I'm going to hide you under a bucket,
> do you? I'm putting you on a light stand. Now
> that I've put you there on a hilltop, on a light
> stand—shine! Keep open house; be generous with
> your lives. By opening up to others, you'll prompt

people to open up with God, this generous Father
in heaven. (Matthew 5:13–16 MSG)

This is red-letter, y'all! (Just in case, red letters in the Bible
mean Jesus said it.) Jesus wants us sprinkling salt everywhere we
go. We found out that if we loved people right where they were
and walked around with a saltshaker, people would want to be in
our community.

So now we have a community of people who gather in the
spirit of love and service. We gather month after month at dinners
for widows and in elementary schools for kids' birthdays. We
gather with like-minded lovers of people.

10

Watch for Falling Pianos

Leah

Why do cartoons featuring pianos falling on unsuspecting victims get a belly laugh from me? Better yet, why does that overplayed and totally improbable scene guarantee big laughs? That piano busting into a billion pieces as it hits that poor person or animal—what a hoot! Don't judge me. I know you laugh at those scenes too.

Here's what I know about life, about my journey with Beautiful Day, and about parenting, marriage, career, trips to Walmart with two hungry kids—whatever. As long as you live, you'll experience falling-piano incidents only they will not be the funny kind on cartoons. You will. I'm quite sure you already have. Pianos of all shapes and sizes fall on us or near us all the time. It's just what happens on earth to our earthly bodies. Life is full of blessings, but wisdom tells us there's another side to that coin. Trials. Troubles. Falling pianos. These words do not need to be scary when we frame them in what Jesus said was true.

> These things have I spoken unto you, that in me ye
> may have peace. In the world ye have tribulation:
> but be of good cheer; I have overcome the world.
> (John 16:33 ASV)

If you are like me, the "ye" in that scripture may make it tough to apply to ye life, but let's do it anyway. You are the ye. You are. I promise. In this world, you will have tribulation. *Webster's* defines tribulation as unhappiness, pain, or suffering. Yep, I've experienced that. Jesus knew that this earth would never provide us with peace. Of course not. He's the only giver of peace. He never intended us to dig around and find peace all by ourselves.

"But be of good cheer" is my favorite part. The amplified version of that verse reads,

> I have told you these things, so that in Me you may
> have [perfect] peace. In the world you have tribulation
> and distress and suffering, but be courageous [be
> confident, be undaunted, be filled with joy]; I have
> overcome the world. (John 16:33 AMP)

I admit that being of good cheer is not my first reaction to a piano falling on or near me. Sweating and panicking are usually my go-tos when that piano has smashed me into the concrete. This good cheer is more of an anchor than an emotion for me. Good cheer in the midst of circumstances. Why? How? I'm glad you asked. In the last part of that verse, Jesus said, "I have overcome the world" (John 16:33 AMP).

Jesus told us this from a place of victory. He said that to His disciples and to ye and me. Pianos may fall. Pianos will fall. But

He has won victory over each one. And if we say yes to Jesus, His victory is ours.

Victory from under that piano is possible. Michele and I have a billion stories about such victories in our journey with Beautiful Day. That program was expanding like crazy in the summer of 2016, and we had a volunteer meeting scheduled in a new school district outside our city limits. These volunteer meetings are a huge deal because they happen only once a year per school district. This is our big moment to pitch the Beautiful Day vision to new souls who are feeling called to join this journey.

That particular volunteer meeting in this new community happened to fall on a night when Michele's and my power crew was unable to attend. One by one, our key people were hit by falling pianos and were unable to dig themselves out before the meeting. So there we were, just Michele and I, packing my car stinkin' full of the Beautiful Day gear needed for this meeting in heat and humidity that only southwestern Oklahoma could generate in June. Sweating hardly describes what my body was doing as we loaded the car. We were prepared. Locked and loaded. One final task before heading to the new school twenty minutes away—pick up a sheet cake from Homeland. In that heat.

Help me, Rhonda.

I was already dressed in my Beautiful Day shirt. My partner in crime … bless her heart. She's not only the cofounder and key visionary of Beautiful Day; she also owns a business. She works a full-time job and carries a heavy Beautiful Day load. We try to keep her capes pressed and dry cleaned. She was still in her work gear as we ran—yes, ran—into Homeland to get that cake. We had no time for anyone. No time for anything. No time! Can you see that piano dangling above us?

When we were nearly to the bakery counter, a voice called out, "Beautiful Day! Look! It's Beautiful Day!"

This tiny thing—maybe nine years old and with a head full of curls—ran to me and wrapped her arms around my sweaty body. My time line melted. My plan to do what it took to get in and out of there as quickly as possible was no longer important. The piano had fallen, but that time, it hadn't hit me. Instead of being trapped under that piano, I stood with this little girl at the deli counter just hugging and remembering my purpose. Remembering what God had invited me to taste and see.

> Taste and see that the Lord is good. Oh, the joys of
> those who take refuge in him! (Psalm 34:8 NLT)

Only Jesus could turn that falling piano into an opportunity right in front of our eyes. We were not looking for it, but it found us. He found us. Jesus always knows where I am.

The longer I walk with the Lord, the wiser I hope to become so I can spot a potential falling-piano day. There are a million different falling-piano scenarios.

- I'm under the piano.
- The piano hit my foot.
- The piano missed me.
- The piano got my buddy.
- The piano smashed my sandwich.

Jesus has overcome this piano-falling world, and I can keep my eyes on Him.

11

Squirrel!

Leah

Have you seen the Pixar movie *Up*? In the movie, a dog is equipped with a collar that gives him the ability to talk with humans. In one scene, the dog jumps on a human he just met and starts talking to him: "My master made me this collar. He is a good and smart master and made me this collar so that I may talk. *Squirrel!* My master is good and smart."

When the dog says "squirrel," there's a long pause before he continues his conversation with this human. Hilarious!

This dog is equipped to do the extraordinary—talk to humans. And he does. But in the middle of exercising his miraculous ability, he is easily distracted because he's an ordinary dog. What makes him extraordinary are his master and what his master created just for him. I'm no Bible scholar, but this movie scene speaks to me. Anyone who says yes to Jesus is equipped to do the extraordinary. Even ye. But being equipped with the extraordinary (this is the Holy Spirit by the way) doesn't make us immune to distractions.

The beauty of Beautiful Day has been its simplicity. Michele and I say it all the time: "It's not complicated. It's simple. The mission of Beautiful Day is simple." Since we started Beautiful Day, we've heard so many cool ideas well-meaning people think we should add to our mission. *Squirrel!* We had some folks suggest that since we have the word *beautiful* in our name, our shirts— our uniforms—should be fancied, blinged up. *Squirrel!* A sweet woman once suggested we make the widows' events quarterly instead of monthly. *Squirrel!*

I'm not saying any one of these ideas is bad or impossible or even difficult; it's just that they're not our missions. Keeping it simple is the key with Beautiful Day. Its simplicity avoids the mission being derailed and becoming overly complicated.

> *Any fool can make something complicated.*
> *It takes a genius to make it simple.*
> —Woody Guthrie

My husband has always loved mission work. He likes a million things about it, and the whole process energizes his soul. Years ago before we had kids, I decided I wanted to go with him on one of his mission trips. I was perhaps jealous of what he was experiencing on his trips, and I badly wanted to experience it with him. So we got our shots. (Well, he got his shots while I ran around the house for two hours crying as Che tried to give me shots.) We packed. We left on our trip. There was no part of that trip that I enjoyed. My being on that trip was the most square-peg-in-a-round-hole event I'd ever experienced.

Have you ever been somewhere that you were absolutely not

supposed to be but yet there you were? That was a squirrel moment for me. I got distracted from my own life trying to make God's mission for Che's life my mission. Going on that mission trip was awesome for Che, but it was not what God had called me to do. I accidentally followed a squirrel to that mission trip.

So if God has a calling for you—and He does—feel free to ask Him about that calling. Wrestle with it, examine it, and make sure you're hearing His voice and not simply a louder, distracting voice. His call for your life is specific and purposeful. There are so many voices to be heard in this world. Don't even get me started on the billions of social media voices flashing in all our faces. My shower—I mentioned it earlier in this book—is such a quiet space for me, and the quiet sets the stage to hear that still, small voice.

> He reveals deep and mysterious things and knows
> what lies hidden in the darkness, though he is
> surrounded by light. (Daniel 2:22 NLT)

Friends, I want to hear, see, and feel these deep and mysterious things! It's a bit scary and risky to pursue such things, but give me risk over lukewarm any day. The plans He has for my life are His plans, and His Word tells me they are plans for my good. Look it up in your Bible. Go see for yourself what His plans are for your life. Read Jeremiah 29:11.

So with Beautiful Day and with other callings in my life, I pray that I seek His voice and let those squirrels run right by me. I can trust Him. I cannot trust those squirrels.

12

That's Gonna Leave a Mark

Michele

My heart. Your heart. All hearts. Don't we all have at least one thing in common? We all have hearts that are battered and bruised. Full of scars. Full of markings. Some fresh, open wounds. And some old wounds with Band-Aids covering the holes left behind.

If you could see my heart, you'd see all sorts of markings on it. While these bruises, wounds, and scars may not be pretty, they're my story. I'm not sure I'd be willing to let go of any of them. Each one of these markings tells a story, and they aren't all bad. These stories are about me and who I am today.

We tend to think of Beautiful Day as a living and breathing organization that has a heart that's no different from any other heart. It's bruised and battered and scarred and all marked up. But we've learned so much from all those markings.

At Kindred Community, we get to meet the coolest ladies and build relationships with them month after month. We show up and serve these precious souls, and somehow, we end up on the receiving end of the relationship. We expected (well, hoped) women to come to these dinners and make friends, but we didn't expect to gain friendships for ourselves. We have been pleasantly surprised over and over with our monthly guests. The love these women pour out to us, the volunteers, is enough to fill the Grand Canyon.

It was June 2015 when we lost our first Kindred Community guest, a widow. That had been on our unexpected list. It had never crossed our minds that we might lose one of our new friends. A group of us walked into that funeral brokenhearted but led by our fearless leader, Jan. I bet there were fifteen of us. We took some aprons in a symbolic effort to serve her one last time. We sat off to the right in the back trying to go unnoticed. The funeral was beautiful. There were one billion flowers and a beautifully made quilt with all her grandchildren's names embroidered on it draped over her casket.

A man came up to us and asked, "Are you all the Beautiful Day ladies?" Stunned, Jan answered, "Yes." He said, "Follow me. The family wants you all sitting in the front."

Wait! What? We can't. We shouldn't. Oh wait. We have to. We will.

After he escorted us to the front, he asked if we had any more aprons. Jan nodded. "Yes. They're in the lobby." He went to the lobby for one. We were paralyzed with tears running down our cheeks as we watched him scoot the custom quilt down to make room for the Beautiful Day apron to be draped over her casket.

Our Beautiful Day heart was receiving a mark. That event marked our hearts in an unforgettable way. Beautiful Day's

Kindred Community for Widows was a part of this woman's life for such a short time, but she had a mark on her heart that read "Kindred Community."

This was a giant eye-opener for us. We realized we were marking people's hearts in good ways. We walked into a funeral hoping to go unnoticed, but we walked out knowing we had made a mark on her life. And she had marked ours.

That's where we are now with Beautiful Day. We're hoping for this all to leave a mark on you and a mark on me and the next one and the next one.

Go leave a mark!

In memory of our friend,
Dorinda Speed
Until we see you again.

13

Say Yes to Piano Lessons

Leah

I turned forty not long ago. What a milestone. I bet I'm the only person ever to turn forty. I treated that milestone more like an accomplishment. As if I'd finally reached this difficult goal I'd been training for for forty years. Then one day it just happened. I woke up and was actually forty.

I had an urge to stretch myself that year. To try new things. I have always wanted to learn to play the piano, but I had had zero musical training (aside from my iTunes). Could a brain that had just turned forty learn something new?

I found a piano teacher willing to teach adults. The day arrived for my first lesson. I was so stinkin' nervous. As the lesson time got closer, I became insanely busy with Beautiful Day business. Pianos were falling all over the place. A million people needing me right then. I stopped and looked at the escape route I knew was available. You know, the escape route that's actually a trap. The escape route that says, "Quick! Get out of there! You can't afford to take on anything new right now! Learning new things at your age is a silly pipe dream. Quick! Escape! Get back to work!"

I turned my back on that trap. As weird as it sounds, I felt God calling me to piano lessons. That still, small voice was saying, "Come over here. I want to show you something cool." This would be an amazing place to tell you that I'm now playing the piano all over the world, winning awards, and wowing music critics. Nope. Though I do play a riveting rendition of "When the Saints Go Marching In." Not a lot of piano greats put a funeral tempo to this song, but it's my jam.

But this part is true: piano is something I'm loving. God really did call me to start taking lessons. Just thirty minutes a week for the lesson and practicing throughout the week. It's the most beautiful private time for me. I can feel myself getting richer because of this—richer for the experience.

Beautiful Day has not collapsed because of my unavailability during those thirty piano minutes a week. Shocking, I know. God designed me to be able to do all He has called me to do. I see people getting burned out all the time doing their God-called missions, but He doesn't intend to burn anyone out with what He asks. On the contrary, His plans offer us all rich, full lives and freedom! But I had to trust that He was calling me, and I had to make sure it was not just a louder, more-distracting voice calling me. His voice has a sweetness to it.

Michele experienced a similar struggle when her Ava wanted to sign up for a basketball league and she wanted Michele to be her coach. That Michele has loads of talents, and one is being a great basketball player. She played a ton in high school and has an excellent coaching ability. Michele took some time to pray about her schedule to see if there was room for coaching a third-grade basketball team. God confirmed He had called her to that.

It was a beautiful basketball season for eight third-grade girls. My Ava played on Michele's team that year, and those girls learned so much more than just basketball. They learned about sharing, encouraging each other, relying on teammates, and being examples of good sportsmanship. (I'll let you guess how they learned that lesson.) God's calling Michele to coach this team in the middle of her busy life had a certain sweetness to it.

You never know what things God will call you to do. I've found that His callings have no specific formula or recipe. His callings will meet you right where you are with the talents you have or have yet to discover. So do it. Say yes to piano lessons or coaching or whatever He asks you to do. I've seen people give up everything for their callings, and I mean everything. They're just dry bones walking through their callings and dragging their severed limbs behind them. I've also seen people just saying no to their callings. Surely in the middle is a better answer—saying yes but keeping our eyes on the Creator of the call so our steps are directed and burnout doesn't occur.

14

Yes! Even a Cupcakery

Michele: I can't image what all this would look like if we hadn't said yes to Kindred Community. We said yes to something new while in the middle of starting something new. By all accounts, the decision to take on a new ministry at that time was a terrible idea. Any professional would have surely said, "No. You cannot add something before your original something is working." But that tender, sweet voice was calling us. "This way. Come this way. Look over here. I have another door you can see behind."

I read once that Jesus operated on a reverse economy—what was first on earth was last in heaven. And that Jesus's ways were not ours.

> "My thoughts are nothing like your thoughts,"
> says the Lord. "And my ways are far beyond
> anything you could imagine." (Isaiah 55:8 NLT)

Leah: I have a deep hunger to be eternity focused, and that focus changes everything. This focus will supernaturally dim the things of this world. In every way, Beautiful Day has proven this true. The way it got started, the people who started it, the intense growth we have experienced and so on.

Being eternity focused is just another way of saying a perspective change. I don't know where my compass was pointed before my mom got sick. Maybe it was pointed somewhere different every day. But today I am different. I'm still me. Human. Flawed. Messy. I am all of that, but I have also tasted and seen for myself the good news, and it's all true. God has a plan for my life, and it's a good plan. He will speak to me and help me. Oh how He loves me.

Michele: Back in that story of being at that Christian Women's' conference is where I first heard Hillsong UNITED's "Oceans" for the first time.

You call me out upon the waters
The great unknown where feet may fail
And there I find You in the mystery
In oceans deep
My faith will stand

And I will call upon Your name
And keep my eyes above the waves
When oceans rise
My soul will rest in Your embrace
For I am Yours and You are mine

Trust is all over this song. Being led by the spirit and not by my flesh. And that my faith would be made stronger by this faithful action. Wow!

I thought I would just have to say yes once; I didn't know it would become a daily thing. Praying that "Oceans" song. Praying it as I worshipped along with the singers on stage. It wasn't thirty minutes later that God asked me to do something for the first time ever. Just as I had asked Him moments before. That meant He had to be listening. I have no doubt He was listening, but I admit I used to wonder if He was. The proof was in the nachos. Pudding. Whatever.

Leah: Had you asked me in that parking lot on August 21, 2013, if I was prepared to help lead a ministry like Beautiful Day that now serves 4,000 kids and 250 widows, I would have given you my dumb-dog look. I'm not sure I would even have answered such a crazy question, but it didn't happen like that. God's ways are not our ways. It was one yes and then another and another. Like boiling a lobster. The water is suddenly boiling when just a few minutes ago it wasn't.

Michele and I swear to this: God has yet to ask us to do something and not given us everything we needed to accomplish His task. Every single time. Our faith has absolutely grown watching all this come together so beautifully. Seeing other people readily answer the call to serve has let us see that we are not the only ones, not by a long shot. There is a Bible verse about God planting eternity in all human hearts found in Ecclesiastes 3:11. I think that's what we've gotten to see firsthand. When the Creator calls and a heart is tuned to hear that call, response happens and the impossible happens.

What if we would have needed total of 40,000 cupcakes

to celebrate all these kids? Can you imagine? Did we forget to mention until just now that a crazy, cool part of Beautiful Day celebrations is that trays of cupcakes are delivered to the birthday kids' classrooms so they can celebrate each other as a class? Yup. That's part of what we are honored and blessed to do. The first year, we needed just 1,000 cupcakes, but that was still a ton of cupcakes as far as we were concerned then. However, by the time we got to our fourth year, our need was for 25,000 cupcakes to celebrate all these amazing kiddos in one year!

But God made a way for us to get 40,000 cupcakes during our first four years. How could that be? God sent a wonderful, sugary, corporate sponsor to meet this impossible need. Duncan Regional Hospital is a facility full of folks who love to say yes.

What's next for us? A Beautiful Day Cupcakery? Could we? Should we? Will we? We don't know. We're still here. And still saying yes.

Remember the Kevin Costner movie *Field of Dreams?* That sweet movie from the '90s made famous the phrase "If you build it, they will come." I like that very much. I used to need all the answers, but the Lord has gently taught me that I don't. He's also taught me that I don't need to know all the questions; I just need to lean into Him. I recognize that sweet voice, and I pray that my answer will always be yes.

Both: The song "Oceans" at the beginning of this chapter beautifully describes the imagery we believe the Lord has given us during our journey. He's been inviting us to step closer to Him way out on this body of water one rock at a time, one step at a time. The first rock wasn't too far from shore, so we clasped hands and jumped to that rock. Let's be honest; we were kind of shocked that we made that leap and even more shocked when the next rock appeared. *More? He has more for us to do? We get to do more?*

Sometimes, the water was smooth and clear; we could see to the bottom. We could see the next rock rising up. Other times, the water was rough and murky and we had to leap those times before we were certain the next rock was even there.

We look back now and still see the land, but we know that if we keep trusting Him, one day, we'll look back and maybe see just a tiny dot of what was once our comfort zone.

The cool thing about this invitation is that it's not just for Michele Johnson and Leah Miller and your pastor and your Sunday school teacher and your mentor and Joyce Meyer and Billy Graham. It's for you. We promise it is. He wants—nope—He's pleading with you to trust Him. He doesn't need us to fulfill His desires; rather, He invites us to come along and see really cool things!

We hope this finds you in a spot where you're being inspired and where you are feeling drawn to your Creator maybe even for the first time. Or maybe you have already said yes but you need encouragement to take the next step or even the first step. Maybe you know God but have drifted from Him and you want to pull up close to Him again. Oh how He wants that too. May you seek Him earnestly and let Him helps you discover His call on your life! The calling that God made you to do!

Contact Us

We would love to hear from you! Reach out to us.

Jon Stone's *There's a Monster at the End of This Book* is such a hoot! Grover, a Sesame Street character, is illustrated all through the book giving silly warnings about reaching the end of the book and the monster that will surely be there. We can relate to Grover's feeling. We weren't sure what we would find at the end of this book-writing journey. Some days, it felt like surely there would be a real live monster at the end of it, but as with Grover's fear, there was no monster. Writing this book was the most fun, scary, hilarious, intimidating, freeing thing we have done together. We hope you have enjoyed being on this journey with us.

We would love to meet you, to hear your next-step stories, or just to connect with you. If you would like to learn more about the Beautiful Day Foundation, please follow our beautiful days at

Website: www.BeautifulDayFoundation.net
Instagram: @beautiful_day_foundation
Facebook: /BeautifulDayFoundation
Twitter: @beautiful_day_foundation
Email: BeautifulDayFoundation2013@yahoo.com

References

Goff, Bob. *Love Does*. Thomas Nelson, 2014.

Hillsong UNITED. "Oceans (Where Feet May Fail)." Zion. By Matt Crocker, Joel Houston, and Salomon Ligthelm, 2013.

Hybels, Bill. *Courageous Leadership*. Zondervan, 2012.

Irish twins. *Merriam-Webster*, www.merriam-webster.com/, accessed September 30, 2016.

Up. Walt Disney Studios Home Entertainment, 2013.

Printed in the United States
By Bookmasters